Vision Board Party 101

Vision Board Party 101
How to Host a Party That Changes Lives

Natasha Gayden

Copyright © 2016 by Natasha Gayden

All rights reserved. This book or any portion thereof

may not be reproduced or used in any manner whatsoever without the express written permission of the publisher except for the use of brief quotations in a book review.

Printed in the United States of America First Printing, 2016

ISBN 978-0-9978898-0-2 (ebook) ISBN 978-0-9978898-1-9 (soft cover)

Elevate Master Coaching LLC.
coach@elevatemastercoaching.com
www.elevatemastercoaching.com

I dedicate this book to God who revealed to me......my vision and allows me to help others' realize the vision in their lives as well.

To my Husband Darick, who drives the Vision for our lives every...single....day. You inspire me and you see me. And I see you...

To my best friend Tomisha, who is the integrity behind the Vision. You help keep my journey honest and fun.

To my Sisters of 20/20 Vision, give thanks to God in advance for what we will accomplish in His name. Each of you is necessary and equipped. Thanks for sharing this journey with me!

Table of Contents

Prologue 7

Vision 9

What is a Vision Board? 11

The Power of the Vision Board 15

Vision Boards Cover Every Area of Your Life 20

    Career and Business 22

    Wealth 24

    Self-Care 25

    Family & Friends 26

    Fun 28

Big Crazy Goals 30

Building Community 33

Tools and Materials Needed 36

    Host Checklist 39

    Icebreakers, Games, and other Shenanigans. 40
    Powerful Women or Women of the Bible
    Icebreaker Game 40

    Get to Know Me Questions 44

Prologue

So you have decided to host a Vision Board Party. Congratulations on becoming one of the great hosts who throw a party with a purpose. And what's the purpose, you may ask? The purpose is Vision. Whether it's setting the Vision, realizing the Vision or celebrating the Vision, you and your guests are in for a delicious treat. Since vision parties came on the scene, many lives have been changed for the better. And you, being the Purpose Driven host that you are, will also contribute to changing lives one vision board at a time.

At one of my parties, several years ago someone invited a 94-year-old woman, we will call Mrs. Lou. I was pretty nervous when I met Mrs. Lou because I thought, "She won't get anything out of these activities. She is retired and probably not seeking to achieve anything." At the end of the party, Mrs. Lou pulled me aside and thanked me for a great time. She then said to me, "I'm 94 years-old, and I haven't dreamed about anything in a long time. But after this party, I realized that as long as I'm living, I can still dream and set goals." She laughed and the said, "I'm about to plan my next five years."

That was a powerful moment for me. By me showing other women the importance of Visioneering, I was helping to impact lives... changing lives. Even the life of a 94 year-old who was done dreaming of a desired life. I have many other stories on the impact these parties have had on the lives of young girls and women. These stories are all very different, yet precious and unique. However, the one thing they all have in common is their lives are changed.

Vision

"Your hand can't hit what your eyes can't see. Float like a butterfly, sting like a bee!"
  – Muhammad Ali

The Great Muhammad Ali understood all too clearly what most people miss in their lives today. He knew that to hit your target, goal or in his case opponent, you first had to see it. This quote makes me think of the meaning of Vision. And I assert," you will never get where you are going until you can see yourself there first."

Vision separates the leaders from the followers. Vision exposes those who are in the game vs. those who are sleepwalking through life. Vision allows us to see a better life, career, health or marriage. The ability to visualize the future life you want in a clear, understandable way is the key to success.

Whether it's one year, three years or five years out, setting a vision for your life is one of the best things you will ever do for yourself. I attest to the Power of the Vision Board. Since I began hosting Vision Board Parties, I went from a mediocre job, hating Mondays and my dreams deferred, to owning my own business. I also started a Non-

Profit to help women, became financially healthy and am now walking in my God-Given Purpose.

Do you want to become more successful? If the answer is YES, start by getting a Vision for your life.

What is a Vision Board?

The most basic definition of a vision board is this: It's a collection of images, quotes, and symbols that have meaning to you and which bring out feelings of joy, peace, love, and happiness. They represent your dream life.

And that's what vision boards are all about. Dreaming.

Rather than a bland calendar, spreadsheet, task list or goal sheet with dates and impressive sounding goals on them, vision boards give you the creativity to let your dreams come alive and grow.

Which is more inspiring to you? This method:

- 7/30/15 – Published Author.
- 8/30/15 – Start French Classes.
- 12/31/15 – Buy New Red BMW. Or this method:

Vision boards come in many different formats, both digital and physical. We'll talk more about that later, but for now, let's take a look at the types of contents that make up vision boards.

Images. This is by far the most common item to find on vision boards; images can be photos, drawings, mind maps, sketches or anything else that has some meaning for you.

For example, if you desire a beach vacation as one of your goals, you might include photos of a beach, beach house, or the ocean (imagine yourself sipping a Piña Colada while lounging in a beach chair). If you dream of owning a home, then a photo of your dream home will serve as a happy reminder of what life will be like when achieving this goal.

Affirmations/Motivational Messages. You've seen those motivation posters that say things such as, "Carpe Diem, Seize The Day!" For some people, these messages can be incredibly powerful. When you face a rough patch, simply remembering that phrase can be enough to get you fighting again.

Your vision board might include messages you see posted on social media, phrases you read and jot down in your journal, testimonials from your clients or nice things others have said about you.

Your Favorite Quotes/Scriptures. Inspiration is different for everyone. For some, the greatest source of inspiration is the Bible. For others, words of encouragement from industry leaders or historical figures is uplifting. You can have fun with these, too. Maybe your best inspiration comes from church signs or a fortune cookie. Whatever makes you smile or brightens your day is a good fit for your vision board.

Everything Else. What else inspires or motivates you? The family Christmas card you sent out last year? The first dollar you made from your business? Your grandma's necklace? Vision boards can include these motivational items and more; you just might have to be a little creative when it comes to adding them.

We'll talk about the materials for creating a vision board in a later section. But first, let's look at the reality of how vision boards can change your life.

The Power of the Vision Board

Vision Boards have transformed many lives and can change your life too. The method of using visualization techniques to map out your goals and dreams is transforming. And isn't this the whole purpose of dreaming in the first place... to change your current situation for the better?

If done correctly, the Vision Board is an excellent tool to help you change your life. If done incorrectly, it just becomes a poster board with images. You must first start your board with a purpose. Ask yourself these Purpose Questions:

1. What are my authentic desires? Do they line up with my purpose?
2. Are my intentions good or well meaning?
3. What am I currently grateful for?
4. What goals will move me forward towards my dreams?
5. What are my dreams?

Once you've interviewed yourself and dig deep down to explore with wisdom, your dreams, and goals, then watch your Vision Board come to life. I cannot stress how important this step is. If you don't self-explore, the chances are that your Vision Board is ego driven. Your Vision Board may also be ego driven if it is primarily about attaining material items. Search out your authentic desires and create a balanced Vision Board that will facilitate lasting change.

The power of the Vision Board also manifests itself in how you feel. Your Vision Board should be designed to inspire and motivate you. You should get a quick dose of energy every time you see it. Having a bad day? Spend some time with your Vision Board to remind you of why everything you go through is worth it. Feeling unaccomplished? Lay out your board and become grateful for all you have already accomplished. Just looking at your Vision Board at any time should help you feel how important you are and how important your dreams are.

A successfully designed Vision Board will help you to achieve your dreams and feel good about yourself. That is the Power of the Vision Board. When you visualize your ideal business, your happy home life, your dream vacation, and even your biggest income goals, you're primed to achieve them. See…. then achieve!

Now that's Powerful!

As a host, it is your role to facilitate the power of the Vision Board. It's not enough for you to simply ask yourself these Purpose Questions. It is important for you to pose these questions to your guests. You can do this by:

1. Creating a theme for your event. This is highly important! The theme sets the tone for the vision and learning which will take place at your event. For example, one year I did a Vision Party theme of "Women of Intention - Walking in Your Purpose." I made sure that all of my materials (games, icebreaker, learning, and gifts) matched my theme.

2. Conducting an icebreaker or play games which incorporate the Purpose Questions.

3. Teaching a lesson around purpose, intentions or whatever personal development content that aligns with your theme.

4. You and others share powerful testimonies with the group which highlights the importance of Purpose Questions.

Through multiple activities and asking the Purpose Questions, you can lead your guests to a greater self-awareness and to begin thinking about and living in their purpose.

The Power of the Vision Board also plays out in the testimonies, the sharing of the wins and opportunities and bonding of the women who attend your party. My favorite part of the Vision Board Party is when I get to hear about all the accomplishments from the previous year. I equally enjoy hearing about the misses and the obstacles as well. The authenticity that is displayed during this portion of the party is refreshing. It gives us an opportunity to encourage each other out in the open. It is not uncommon for the women to yell out support to each other, through scriptures, affirmations, congratulations and big loving hugs. It is also not uncommon to experience tears of joy and tears of pain from your guests. As a host who is committed to their guests' experience, it is important to ensure the following:

1. Create an environment where people feel open to share their thoughts, feelings, wins and losses.
2. Eliminate distractions, such as music, TV or people talking, when someone is sharing their stories.
3. Be sure you are attentive and encourage your other guests to do the same when someone is speaking.
4. Make sure not to provide your opinion or try to give advice to the person who is speaking. This is a share only exercise. Please be sure to tell your guests this as well.

I have found the easiest way to ensure the above items are followed is by making an announcement with ground rules before anyone speaks. This way, there is no confusion. The worst thing that can happen when someone is up speaking is the audience is talking, disruptive or making fun of the speaker. As a host, you have to manage this and ensure everyone feels safe to share. When the environment is safe, you truly get to know each other and how to help each other as a Sisterhood. And when your sister laughs, you laugh. When she cries, you cry with her. When she is ready to go to war, you are by her side. And when she is winning, she makes sure YOU are winning, too. Vision Board parties usher in Sisterhood.

Now what's more Powerful than that?

Vision Boards Cover Every Area of Your Life

Before we get into how vision boards can affect all the aspects of your life, let's take a minute to look at the most common mistake people make when creating them:

They focus on the actual goal rather than the result.

Imagine you have a goal of visiting Paris. You could express that by just writing "Paris" on a whiteboard. But so what? The word itself is unlikely to evoke feelings of joy or anticipation. In fact, the more you see that word, the less meaning it will have.

As a vision board item, it's pretty weak.

Imagine instead, a photo of the Eiffel Tower. It's nighttime, and the tower is glowing bright yellow on the Seine River. You can almost hear the voice of a Jazz singer with her symphonic band in tow. You can see yourself in a glass boat with the Eiffel Tower in view, as you cruise down the Seine River in Paris with the one you love.

When you look at the picture, it doesn't just say, "Paris." It instantly transports you there and immerses you in the moment. It's a feeling. Not a goal.

When you create your vision board, regardless of which of life's aspects you're focusing on, be sure to look for images and words that make you feel the way you imagine you'll feel when you achieve your goal. It's not about what you want to have. It's about how you want to feel.

Career and Business

Career and Business goals are probably the most common topic of vision boards, and rightfully so. People view a direct correlation of the station in life with their career and business success. So they set goals around their careers and business with the intent to create a better life for themselves or their family.

Vision boards are the perfect choice to help reach their desired goals.

When you're building your business vision board, consider the following questions:

- How do I want my day to go?
- How much revenue do I want to bring in?
- What does my ideal client look like?
- How many employees will I have?
- What do I want my business to look like by the end of the year?
- What will my office look like?

When you're building your career vision board, consider the following questions:

- What do I want a typical workday to look like?

- How much money do I want to make per year?
- What skills/education do I need to obtain to move forward?
- What will my office look like?
- What awards do I want to win?

Look for images and other items that represent your ideal career or business day, your perfect client, and your ultimate dream job.

Wealth

Wealth, wealth, wealth!!! Everybody wants to be wealthy. So that makes this another favorite topic for vision boards. If becoming wealthy is one of your big dreams, then it's one area you should pay close attention to.

Being wealthy is a mindset, first and foremost. I have studied many people who are very wealthy, and they all had one thing in common; they believed that they could reach their dream. The reason many people don't reach their dreams is that they let those negative internal voices hold them back. You know that voice. It says things like:

- "You'll never earn that much."
- "No one will pay you to do that."
- "You've always been financially irresponsible, and you always will be."
- "You're just not 'good' with money."
- "They'll never accept that price increase."

We let these voices hold us back, and unless we take steps to silence them, we will never earn what we're truly worth.

A well thought out vision board can help. Begin by asking yourself...

- What does financial freedom mean to me?
- How can I educate myself about savings and debt?
- Exactly how much money do I want to have in my bank account at the end of XX?
- What bills do I want to be paid off by xx?
- How can I change the world if I earn more money?
- What charities will I support when I start earning xx?

Then find the pictures that are distinct reminders of what you want to achieve financially. Find a picture of the place(s) you plan to visit when you retire. Or, how about a big pile of money so that you can retire young and live on a yacht. It's your dream, and it can be anything you want it to be.

The point is, your vision board is the perfect conduit for finally silencing that negative voice in your head that's keeping you from your financial goals.

Self-Care

How's your physical health? How's your mental health? Let's be honest, for many on the go women, Moms, and career women, it could be better.

We spend all of our time making sure that others are cared for and allow little time for our own wellness. We don't eat properly. We struggle to find time to exercise. And stress is winning the war in our lives. We say that our health is a priority. However, we put ourselves last and battle to meet our self-care goals. The truth is, we have real intention in the area of self-care, but often abandon our goals in the pursuit of helping others.

How can a vision board help? By helping, you visualize what good health **looks** like and **feels** like. One year, I put this saying on my vision board, "Nothing taste as good as being healthy feels." This quote helped me to see what feeling good looks like. You can use an image of a woman peacefully meditating. Or use a before and after image of someone who has lost weight to motivate you towards your goals.

As with any area, let the vision board guide you to a healthier life that focuses on self-care.

Family & Friends

For me, this is where I start my vision board. I start with goals around my family life, relationship goals between me and my husband or building and strengthening relationships with others. I place my images in the center of my vision board because this area is most important to me. Many people don't put family and friend goals on their vision board because they don't know how to make them measurable.

Creating a family and friends vision board can change that. Ask yourselves these questions:

- What kind of relationships do I want to have?
- What type of friend do I want to be?
- What's most important to me as a Wife? Mother? Daughter? Friend?
- What meaningful touch points do I want to have with my family? Friends?
- How do I want my husband to *feel* when he sees me?
- How do I want my kids to *feel* when they're teenagers?

Fill your vision board with items that represent the best relationships you can imagine, and soon enough, you will see the bonds grow stronger in all of your relationships.

Fun

As the host of several successful Vision Board Parties, I learned that fun is the key to success and engagement. You must ensure you put a lot of thought into having fun, or your vision party will be a bust. Imagine hosting a party where you spend 2-3 hours, posting pictures and writing affirmations on a vision board. It will get the job done. However, imagine hosting a party where people are up moving around, laughing, getting to know each other, and sharing life stories. Which one of those parties would you rather host? Which party do you believe changes lives?

I use several vehicles to incorporate fun into my parties. I use Icebreakers to get us going and I use games to drive competition amongst the women. Women can be extremely competitive when good gifts are the prize. The competitive spirit is great because I use it to get the women at my parties to step outside of their comfort zones. Most people hate speaking in front of a crowd. I design all of my icebreakers and games to require them to speak in front of the other women. I have been known to create crazy games that cause my guests to be silly and not take themselves too serious. For instance, I once did a game where I asked the women to create their own Super Hero names and then make a group commercial to introduce themselves. One year, I had the women create a couture dress out of brown paper bags and decorative tape. Then they had to describe the dress in detail and walk the runway. Can you imagine the craziness and laughter that came out of these games? Fun games create priceless memories. I keep those memories alive by videotaping the games and taking lots of pictures. As a host, you should create as much fun as possible.

Please see the index area for more ideas on how to facilitate fun.

Big Crazy Goals

(Only for the High Performers Who Can't live with the Status Quo. Everyone Else Read at your own risk....)

I love that old saying, **"If your goals and dreams don't make you scared, then they aren't big enough."**

Here's where many of us fail. We sell ourselves short on our aspirations out of fear. So we set a few goals. We set goals we can either easily reach or that other people would consider respectable. Want to increase your income by 20%? Or run in a 5k? Or vacation in Paris?

These are all fine, respectable goals, worthy of your vision boards. But what if you turn them up a notch... or three?

Instead of increasing your income by 20%, increase it by 200%. Rather than running a 5k, compete in a triathlon.

Instead of a vacation in Paris, move there.

With your vision board populated with meaningful images, thoughtful and motivating quotes, inspirational messages, and plenty of creativity, even these big scary goals suddenly feel much more attainable. Within your grasp!

And you know what? As we said earlier, **that which you can visualize, you can achieve.**

So don't be afraid to start a vision board for your biggest, most intimidating goals. You might not get there tomorrow or even next month, but if you keep your FOCUS, you will get there.

Here's my strategy for achieving BIG Crazy Goals:

1. I choose a layup goal- Something I plan to hit which doesn't take too much effort. The reason for doing this is to rev up my energy by achieving a win quickly.

2. I then create what I call "stretch goals". These goals are hard to reach, but not out of my grasp. I suggest that 80% of your goals be stretch goals. If you are achieving these hard to reach goals consistently, chances are you are winning.

3. Finally, I set at least 2 Big Crazy Goals! And guess what? Over the past five years, I've achieved 8 out of the 11 Big Crazy Goals I set. That's a 73%-win rate for goals and dreams that I felt were out of my reach. I'll take those odds any day because the opposite of not creating Big Crazy Goals and going after them is staying stuck where you are or moving very slowly.

So it's up to you…. Create slow moving, easily reached goals or throw in some Big Crazy Goals and accelerate your progress. The choice is yours.

Host: You should encourage Big Crazy Goal setting by modeling this on your Vision Board and in the personal development section of your party. Regardless of what the theme is for your party, it should ALWAYS provide a component of being inspirational and setting aspirational goals. You will find the following as you host these party's year over year:

1. YOU will personally achieve things you never dreamed of in your life. Your achievement will happen because you set a vision for your life first and foremost. You will stand in front of your guests and have the courage to go over your board before they even begin to make their boards.

2. Your Guests will model your behavior and begin creating Big Crazy Goals for themselves. Some will do this successfully; others will take some time getting their stride. No worries! **The goal is to get people to dream big with no limitations.**

3. After setting goals this way, YOU and YOUR GUESTS will begin challenging each other, thinking bigger and dreaming higher. When this happens, lives start to change.

Building Community

When I began hosting vision board parties several years ago, I had no idea how important building a community of supportive women would be in the future. My first party was with ten women who I knew intimately. Each year it grew by at least double digits just by word of mouth. However, as we grew, there became a need for additional support for the women as we tried to navigate through our goals all year. Everyone gets all excited about achieving their dreams during the party and a few weeks after, but then life hits, and the excitement slowly slips away. I became challenged as host and leader of my Vision Movement to keep the comradery of the women, keep the excitement going, and provide some accountability for those who desired it. So I created a tribe or community of women who faithfully attended the vision board parties and are committed to personal improvement. That community is now 500 plus women, and still growing. All by word of mouth.

I learned to build an active community of women by using Facebook Events and Groups. I use Facebook Events to invite women to my Vision Board Party. The event invite also allows my guests to invite other guests. Everything you need guests to know regarding your party can be housed in your event. I used the event invite to update my guests on instructions, changes to the event, and posts to get them excited about our party ahead. Guests are also allowed to post questions and get in on the countdown to party time fun. This vehicle served me well for years until I learned about Facebook Groups.

Facebook Groups is my go-to vehicle for building a community of dynamic women, get it done, sold out to vision Sisters. We are called Women With 20/20 Vision. Facebook Groups allows me to do all of those things I mentioned that the events function does and much, much more. The Facebook Event Page disappears from your view when the event is over, whereas the Facebook Group is forever. I am allowed to build community with these women in a private group that move our visions forward. We hold each other accountable, boost each other up, share our wins and resources, laugh, cry, and pray for each other. We are truly a sisterhood. We even came together and launched a Non-Profit Organization called Women With 20/20 Vision Inc. Our non- profit seeks to empower and advance the quality of life for underprivileged girls and women who strive to become Girl Bosses, seek advanced education, and those who positively impact other women or excel in their lives. We do this by providing funds and scholarships to women who want to advance their studies, start or expand their business. Not only are we pressing to achieve our goals, but we are also now helping other women do the same by providing much-needed resources. Facebook Groups helped me to build this community. As a host, I suggest you use one if not both of these vehicles to build your community of Visioneers as well. Then watch your group soar!

Tools and Materials Needed

So, now that we know what a vision board can do for you and your guests' lives, let's talk about the actual building blocks.

Creating a vision board can be as simple as cutting photos out of a magazine and tacking them up on your office bulletin board, or it can be as complex as a hand-made frame with personal pictures and trinkets. My preference is the Physical method. However, I encourage you to create whatever version that works for you.

- Digital: Created with software designed for the task, or with Photoshop or some other image-editing tool. Ease of use is the obvious benefit of this kind of vision board because you can quickly add and edit your board.

- Physical: Paper, poster boards, whiteboards, or even a wall in your home with hanging pictures. Your creative options are endless here, but your vision board will obviously be less portable.

- Mobile: Created on an app made for tablets and phones. The advantage here is that you'll have your vision board with you everywhere you go.

Remember when you were a kid in art class? Your vision board materials can be just as much fun, especially if you're creating a physical board to hang on your wall. As a host, it is your job to either have the materials needed on hand or explicitly instruct your guests on what materials they will need for the party.

Start by gathering up a selection of materials to work with:
- Swatches of fabric and ribbon
- A stack of old magazines- I collect them all year long
- Colored pencils and markers
- Construction paper
- Poster board- Some have decorative borders
- Crayons
- Stick glue and tape
- Scissors
- Fun stickers and numbers

Instruct your guests to begin to flip through the magazines. The goal is to find images, photos or sayings that make them feel good. Tell them to ask themselves these questions:

Do they make you happy? Do you smile at a particular shot? Does it bring to mind a particular goal or dream? Cut out the images that speak to you in some way.

Tell your guests not to worry about organizing them or categorizing them at this point. For now, they should just make a stack of images that have meaning for them.

Next, have them take their board and do whatever the heck it is they want to do with it!!! Remember, it's their board, their dreams. Encourage them to be as creative as they want to be. This is where you play host extraordinaire and ensure that your guests are full and having fun. **It is important to note that I suggest you create your vision board before your event so that your focus will be on your guests' experience.** I have tried creating my board during the party; however, I found that I am a more effective host when I am free to focus on others.

Make sure that your guests understand that having this tool in their arsenal makes it much more likely they will achieve their dreams, as well as virtually ensuring that their dreams will be larger than they were before they began your vision board hosting adventure. If hosted correctly, your vision board party will change lives. So jump in head first and heed the instructions of an experienced host. My instructions are carefully thought out and purposeful.

But most importantly, and I can't stress it enough... just have fun.

Host Checklist

- [ ] I have my Vision Board completed, and I have asked myself the Purpose Questions:
- [ ] I have communicated to my guests the following:
    - [ ] Sent out Invites at least one month in advance
    - [ ] The Theme of the Vision Party
    - [ ] The materials needed
- [ ] Materials necessary for the event (host provided or guest brought)
    - [ ] Magazines and Pictures
    - [ ] Markers, crayons or colored pencils
    - [ ] Clothing material or swatches
    - [ ] Poster Board (any kind, any color)
    - [ ] Stick Glue or Tape
    - [ ] Scissors
    - [ ] Cut out numbers and fun stickers
    - [ ] Affirmations or Scriptures
- [ ] I have posted my new vision boards in a place where my guests can see it when

they walk in the door.
- ☐ I have snacks, refreshments or light hors d'oeuvres for my guests
- ☐ I have fun icebreakers and games
- ☐ I am ready to host a Vision Party that will change lives!

Icebreakers, Games, and other Shenanigans

Powerful Women or Women of the Bible Icebreaker Game

Items needed- Blank Paper, Markers, and Tape

Time Needed- 20 minutes for Icebreaker, 30 Minutes for the Game

How to play-

The host will choose which theme they want to use- a **Powerful Women, Celebrity Women or Women of the Bible**

Please be sure to select ONE THEME and don't mix. It will be confusing to talk about women of the Bible and celebrity women in the same game.

The host will write a name of a women representative of their chosen theme on a blank sheet of paper with the marker. Please have this done before the event.

When you are ready to begin the game, give the following instructions to your guests.

Each of you will have a name taped on your back. Do not look at the name. Instruct your guests not to tell anyone else of the name taped on their back either.

Ask guests to mingle through the crowd asking questions to try and figure out who is on their back. Each guest will go up to another guest, introduce themselves and ask them **no more than two** questions.

Example:

Hi, My Name is Natasha Gayden, what's your name?

Two questions: Is the women she in the new testament or old testament? Was she one of the disciples?

OR

About how old is she? What is she known for?

If the guest guesses correctly, then ask them to move to the side and wait until everyone figures out their name. If she doesn't guess correctly, then she will move to the next guest and introduce herself and ask no more than two different questions. Each guest will continue this cycle until they guess the answer.

Once all of the guests have their answers, have them introduce themselves to the entire group (name only) and then tell us about the women they have been given. You will find they will struggle to tell you a lot about some of these women, especially Women of the Bible. Don't worry because the game is not over.

Tell your guests the game is not over. Instruct them to use their smartphones to find out more about the woman they have. Tell them at the end of the event; everyone will have a chance to teach the group about their woman. After the presentations, no more than 1 minute per person, the entire group will vote on who gave the best presentation. The winner will get a big prize.

Note: The benefit of this icebreaker/game is the women get to mingle, they have to present, and they end up learning more about powerful women who are important.

The Pocket/Purse Game - 20 minutes

Everyone selects one (optionally two) items from their pocket or purse that has some personal significance to them. They introduce themselves and do a show and tell for the selected item and why it is important to them.

The Talent Show – 45 minutes

Everyone selects one talent or special gift that they possess and can demonstrate for the group. They introduce themselves, explain what their special talent is, and then perform their special talent for the group.

Map Game – 20 minutes

Hang a large map of the world. Give everyone a pushpin. As they enter, they pin the location of their birth on the map or place they most would like to visit. Do not mix themes. Do one or the other.

Don't Drop the Ball- 20 minutes

Stand in a circle with your guests. Use a beach ball to throw around each other. The goal of this exercise is to NOT drop the ball. Throw the ball around to each other continuously. If a person drops the ball, then they are out and must sit to the side. The game continues until the last person standing has never dropped the ball. This game should be played at the end of the party. The purpose of this game is to remind everyone to not drop the ball on what they have learned and the goals they committed to achieving.

Get to Know Me Questions

Items Needed- Scissors and a Bowl Time Needed- 20 Minutes

Cut each square apart and place in a bowl for guests to pull from.

Ask each guest to pick a question out of the bowl as they enter the party. Tell them to think about their question because they will have to answer it later.

When you are ready for your icebreaker, go around and ask each guest to answer their questions. It will be a blast!

What story in your family should be preserved?	Tell us about your favorite day ever.	Who is your favorite person in the world? Why?	What are you looking forward to this year?	What is your greatest disappointment?
If you weren't afraid and could do anything in the world, what would it be?	What TV family is like your family? Explain.	If you could have any super power, what would it be and why?	What is your most embarrassing moment?	What is something new you want to learn?
What is your favorite movie and why?	What are you most thankful for today?	What does the perfect day look like for you?	If you could go anywhere in the world to visit, where would it be and why?	What was your favorite game to play as a child and why?
What is special about your family?	What is your secret fear?	What are three things you can't live without?	What was the best advice you have ever received?	What is the biggest lesson you have ever learned?

Printed in Great Britain
by Amazon